NATIVES

I0140528

Janet Neipris

BROADWAY PLAY PUBLISHING INC
224 E 62nd St, NY, NY 10065
www.broadwayplaypub.com
info@broadwayplaypub.com

First printing July 2011
I S B N: 978-0-88145-465-9

Book design: Marie Donovan
Page make-up: Adobe Indesign
Typeface: Palatino
Printed and bound in the U S A

NATIVES was originally produced by The Invisible Theater in Tucson (Susan Claassen, Managing Artistic Director; James Blair, Associate Artistic Director) with the generous support of Dr Bella Eibensteiner, opening on 20 February 2008. The cast and creative contributors were:

VIOLA .... Susan Claassen
EMILY .... Jillian Courtney
BO .... Natalie Sutherland
GARY .... Eddie Young
JOANNA .... Dallas Thomas
ARNOLD .... Alex Garday
AVERY .... Burney Starks

Director .... Gail Fitzhugh
Producers .... Susan Claassen & Cathy Johnson
Company stage manager .... Hank Krowicki
Set design .... James Blair & Susan Claassen
Light design .... Franklin Calsbeek, Jr
Prop design .... Hank Krowicki
Sound design .... Gail Fitzhugh
Hair & make-up design .... Franki Levin
Technical director .... James Blair
Costume design .... Shana Nunez

CHARACTERS & SETTING

VI, *the mother, 50s**
EMILY, *oldest daughter, 30, teacher of ethnic dance*
BO, *middle daughter, 28, food writer*
GARY, BO's *husband and co-food writer*
JOANNA, *youngest daughter, 26, commodities broker*
ARNOLD, *a sultan from Bali*
AVERY, *50s, black, documentary film maker*

**VI* *can be 60 and the daughter's ages adjusted accordingly to production casting*

Time: *Late Sunday afternoon, June, the present*

Place: *New York City Greenwich Village*

Native: "To be a resident of one's own country"

ACT ONE

(A brownstone, overflowing with books and artwork, eclectic, but in good taste. The owner is clearly a collector. There's lots of Indonesian batiks, African masks, Chinese warriors, New Guinea fishing spears, baskets and pottery. Any furniture is spare and simple, with a studied natural look. The representation of the Living Room is D S, Dining Area U S R, leading to a kitchen, which is not in view. Indication of a few stairs leading to the bedrooms. Some packing boxes are on the floor, mostly filled. VI enters—rather backs in, in slacks, silk shirt, with briefcase, groceries, and stops.)

VI: *(Out front)* I'm the mother, and I admit it. I'm *guilty*. *(Beat Putting down all)* My name is Viola. I was named for an instrument in the New York Philharmonic and conceived the night my parents went to a concert. My mother fell in love with my father during the second movement of the Vivaldi *Viola* Concerto in D-Minor. *(Beat)* Sometimes I feel my entire life is in D-minor. *(Beat)* A lot of what's hanging on the walls is from my daughter Emily. She studies ethnic dance and folklore. She doesn't actually *do* it; she *analyzes* it. Emily travels around the world and sends me things, like this rainstick filled with the bones of a sacred warrior. *(Taking rainstick off the wall, shaking it)* Emily was, at the time, involved with a sultan. She had just returned from Indonesia.

(EMILY enters, loaded down with baggage, woven Indonesian bags, silver bracelets up her arm.)

*(Note: all scenes should flow into each other with no
blackouts. characters exit simultaneous with others entering,
seamless and overlapping.)*

EMILY: *(Putting down her baggage)* I don't believe it! I
don't believe it! I think I have a goddamn parasite!

VI: Emily! What are you doing home? Why didn't you
call? The living conditions sounded dreadful over
there. And al that lemon grass couldn't have been good
for you either. *(Beat)* Did you say something about a
parasite?

EMILY: I've never been so nauseous in my life; and in
three weeks I'm due in Cambridge to do a workshop.

VI: *(Hugging her)* Perfect timing. In three weeks I leave
for France. I've sublet my apartment and rented a
farmhouse in Provence for the summer. God am I
happy to see you!

EMILY: *(Lying down on the couch)* I can feel the little
creatures crawling in and out of my intestines. You
know you can die from parasites. They say once
you have them, you never get rid of them. Probably
pass them on to your children, <u>if</u> you ever have any,
providing your vital organs aren't totally eaten up first.

VI: *(Out front)* This was the summer they all came
home. You've heard of the movement. The return of
the natives. Going back to your roots. It's something
like a root canal. Only it's not covered by insurance. All
three of mine were in "struggle and crisis". They were
turning practically thirty, their leases were up, and
they weren't sure where they were going or coming.
(Beat) It turned out <u>I</u> knew. I first heard about it on
Oprah. They were coming home.

EMILY: I swear I can feel them multiplying.

VI: *(Getting phone, punching numbers)* That's it! I want
you here until you're cured.

EMILY: That's what I hoped you'd say.

VI: Antibiotics and they'll flush it right out of you. *(Into phone)* An appointment for tomorrow, please. *(Beat)* This *is* a parasitic emergency. Emily Davidson. Thank you. *(Puts down phone, then to* EMILY*)* Best doctor of tropical medicine, Kevin Hill. His specialty is disasters. Two o'clock tomorrow.

(Lights down on EMILY. *Spot up on* BO *and* GARY *with Vuitton luggage and lots of it, His and Hers Computers, straw hats, dark glasses. They are dressed like people who are returning from a tropical island)*

BO: Surprise! *(Kissing* VI*)* And I know. We're supposed to be in Cancun.

But who in their right mind goes to Mexico, even if they're giving it away, which now I understand why. We couldn't write a word there.

GARY: And we can't work in Berkeley. Our house is a renovation disaster, workmen everywhere.

BO: So we decided New York was the perfect city to work in.

GARY: Everyone is so driven here.

BO: Can you believe, two of these bags are *just* our research books on native seafood. We stopped in Baltimore to test the crabcakes.

GARY: The reason Copsey's crabcakes are *out*standing is they use blue crabs and just a "trace" of crumbs for binding.

BO: I disagree. It's not the crumb trace; it's the lacing of pepper.

GARY: Their coleslaw, however, was pallid.

BO: It was not. It was tart.

GARY: A trifle tart.

BO: *(To* VI*)* Where should we put our stuff? You're a saint to put us up on short notice.

VI: How about *no notice*? But what else is a mother for? Don't answer that. You can use the guest room.

*(*GARY *exits with luggage.)*

VI: *(Out front)* Bo and Gary are food critics. Bo's the middle daughter. She changed her name from Barbara when she moved west to start her career as a muffin maker, *after* Wellesley, Class of '87. She met Gary in Seattle. He was a cook at a Juice Bar, Brown, Class of '85. Together they took their education on the road and became foodies. Barbara...Bo.. she gets crazy when I call her "Barbara" ...claims it's because as a child she was forced to take over the cooking because I wasn't home, i.e., working. She and her sisters, according to Bo, had had it up to here with spaghettio's. Gary just plain loves food. ... None of us like Gary. He's kind of a prick. *(Then, turning to* BO*) It's you and Gary.*

BO: We're fine.

VI: No you're not. I'm your mother. We know these things.

BO: So he sometimes cares more about rack of lamb than me. It's probably natural for a food critic.

VI: Is it sex? It's always sex.

BO: He reads cookbooks in bed and insists Muffy sleep with us. Muffy's an old dog and she's getting incontinent.

VI: I knew it. Something's wrong between you.

BO: And remember how Gary was a vegetarian? Well, he's become a carnivore. Ribs, pork chops, whole sides of beef. *(Beat)* If I could just stay 'till I get my head together...

VI: It's going to be chaotic here, with me packing and planning your sister Joanna's wedding.

BO: But you know me. I thrive on chaos.

VI: Good, because guess who else is home, back from sunny Indonesia.

BO: Emily! Where is she? *(Calling, looking around the house)* Emily, you bum! Where are you? Not one postcard in a year! EMILY!
  Come out wherever you are!

VI: In the loo, throwing up. She thinks she picked up a parasite in Bali.

(EMILY enters. BO rushes to hug her.)

BO: It's been a whole year!

EMILY: Did you get the drum I sent from New Guinea? Titi made it himself from the skin of a rattlesnake.

VI: *(Out front)* Titi is the Sultan who Emily lived with in Bali while she was studying dance. Titi was originally Arnold Mitterman from the Bronx, and how he got to be a Sultan is another story. They lived together in what was once his palace; but it had fallen on hard times, as had Arnold the Sultan. Emily said they lived off the land. My daughter is a pioneer.

EMILY: Did you hear about Mother? She's moving to France.

VI: Don't I wish. I've sublet my apartment and leased a house in Provence. Finally, I'm going to start my second novel.

BO: But when are you leaving?

VI: Three weeks from today. *(Holding up her compact computer)* My new laptop. *(Pointing to a box)* My notes. My Edith Piaf C Ds.

BO: You've rented our home to a total stranger?

VI: A symphony director.

BO: A perfect stranger will be sitting in our bathtub?

VI: Correction. A respected symphony conductor will be sitting in our bathtub; but Toscanini or not, I'm packing the valuables. *(Continuing to pack)* In France I'll write, I'll live on cheese and wine, I'll hike the hills....

EMILY: You *hike*?

VI: Not exactly, but men hike and I'm single. *(Beat)* He's dating a woman, you know. The American dream. Your father's nabbed himself a doctor.

BO: Be fair, Mother. She's only a dermatologist.

VI: And he's taken up flying; the same man whose idea of adventure was a Ramada Inn on the Jersey shore.

EMILY: He's working on himself. *You're* the one who didn't like him like he was.

VI: Face it. I was married to a man who didn't know Puccini from a porcini mushroom.

GARY: *(Entering)* The porcini mushroom was cultivated by the Medicis, known for the sophistication of their palates.

VI: *(Out front)* One parasite, one incontinent dog, and two not-so-happy daughters. Although I was holding some aces in my hand, the promise of this summer began to be in jeopardy. And this was *before* Arnold the Sultan arrived at our door. But that's much later.

(Light down, spot up on JOANNA.*)*

JOANNA: Phyl and I want a simple Thanksgiving wedding, pumpkins and turkeys and stuff.

VI: We'll have to find a Rabbi and a Minister who will do it together.

JOANNA: Phyl's parents are from Kentucky. They're horse people. They want to come help plan the wedding before you leave. Kind of an engagement party.

VI: *(Statement as question)* Here in New York. In this apartment.

JOANNA: Oh, Phyl's parents adore New York! To them it's *mythological*.

VI: Okay. I'll do it. How many times does a daughter get married? Don't answer that. *(Out front)* But I'm getting ahead of myself. *(Beat)* So it came to pass, in this glorious summer, finally, I was free. Mother dead, father gone, first husband, "bye bye", tenure granted, therapy done *(Pause)* maybe, children grown, gone, packing my bags, my notebooks, my laptop, packing for the little town of Noves, which means "new". This is how I pictured my summer in Provence. The town would be small and have a boulangerie where I'd buy my baguette every morning, and a boucherie, and the butcher would call me mademoiselle, and tell me when the quail eggs were fresh.

   Mornings I'd write by an open window looking over a field of rolled haystacks. Afternoons, I'd read, and on hot days, swim in the river. On rainy days, I'd nap in a single bed, like a nun. *(Beat)* My new novel, I thought, would be about unexpected love late in life. *(Beat)* And one more thing. I would not be alone there. People, even mothers, can have secrets.

(Fade. then lights up. Half an hour later. EMILY, GARY, BO, *and* VI, *glasses in hand)*

VI: *(Holding up her glass in a toast)* To summer! And THIS APARTMENT IS RENTED. Well that's how I'm paying for France… And I feel awful, but I have a date tonight… Well how could I know you'd all be here? We have opera tickets.

GARY: Nicholas?

VI: Nicholas went back to the wife he said he didn't
have. This is *Larry*. We're going to *Aida*. He loves
the part where the elephants come on and you keep
worrying they're going to do their thing on stage.
(Beat) At a hundred dollars a ticket you don't want me
to tell him I can't go? *(Silence, beat)* …. You do.

EMILY: Look, the last thing we want is to interrupt your
life. Just go on as though we aren't here, *like normal*.

VI: "Normal", frankly, escapes me. And if Joanna calls,
say everything's under control. I just pray Phil's not
religious. I don't want all that "Praise be to Jesus" stuff
in the ceremony.

EMILY: *(To VI)* Have you met Phyl yet?

VI: He's coming for the engagement dinner this week
with his parents… Has anyone?

EMILY: What?

VI: Met him.

BO: Kind of.

VI: So?

GARY: Intelligent.

BO: Sophisticated.

GARY: Excellent appetite.

VI: Why am I always the last to know?

EMILY: Maybe because you expect so much.

VI: *(Out front)* A week later Bo and I were planning the
menu for what I thought would be the engagement
dinner.

*(VI picks up a cookbook from the book shelve, BO enters
reading a cookbook)*

VI: I hate it. A fiancé I've never seen, his parents, the Presbyterian horse people, and you know what a dreadful cook I am.

BO: Gary and I will be happy to cook. For us it's like sex.

VI: Thank God. I've been obsessing about this damn dinner. *(Beat)* He tried to put his hand up my dress.

BO: Who tried?

VI: Larry. When we went to the opera, during the stampede.

BO: I don't want to hear this, Ma. Wear slacks next time.

VI: He also French kissed me and I nearly choked. He has this gigantic tongue.

BO: Why are you telling me this? You're supposed to be my mother.

VI: I'm trying to be close.

BO: Then ask me how *I* am.

VI: You've asked me not to be intrusive.

BO: *Now* you may intrude. *(Beat)* I need you to intrude. *(Beat)* I *hate* food. I'm a food writer and I hate food. My whole history… Be a good girl and you can have a brownie. Eat your carrots. They're good for your eyes. Did you ever see a rabbit wearing glasses? In High School, wannagoout for a pizza? Taco Bell? Big Mac? Then along comes Gary and it's "Whatsfordinner?" before I'd even had my morning coffee. And this was when he was still a vegetarian. Steamed barley, bouquets of brussels sprouts. *Then*, when it started to get *really* serious between us, *(Imitating* GARY*)* "Excuse me, but do I detect a jigger of ginger in that couscous?" *(Getting angrier)* I've had it up to here with herbed goat cheese and foccacia.

VI: You don't like Gary anymore.

BO: I don't think I'm in love with him. Maybe I was never in love with him. *(Beat)* After we finish the Folk Food book we've decided to separate..

VI: Where would you go?

BO: I don't know.

VI: *(Out front) I* knew.

(EMILY enters.)

EMILY: I don't believe it! Doctor Hill said it's *not* a parasite, but it *could be* an amoeba.

(Getting a dictionary off the bookshelf)

Amoeba ... *(Reading)* ... a single celled aquatic protozoan with a constantly changing shape, causing infection and dysentery.

(Banging shut the dictionary)

He gave me more tests.

BO: How do you feel?

EMILY: Bilious

BO: Then you're okay. That's how an amoeba's supposed to feel.

EMILY: Sure. Because you *want* me to be okay. You can't bear my getting attention. You never could.

BO: Get real, Em. Someone who studies *The Dancers of Sumba*. No crabcake's ever going to beat that.

EMILY: Is it my fault the men of Java wear *only* a long piece of cloth, hanging down the front covering their whoosie-whatsises when they do the famous horse-trance dance, riding black horses.?

VI: *(Out front)* This was the same summer the Baseball season was almost cancelled and Jackie Onassis was already dead. It did not bode well. *(Turning to* EMILY *and* BO) I don't see why you two have to still be so competitive.

BO: We're siblings. We're *supposed* to be rivals. We're fighting over you, Mum. You're the prize.

VI: What do you do once you get me? Barbecue me in some exotic ceremony while you chant in a circle?

   Still, I'm glad you girls are home. In a way, I missed all the brouhaha. I mean, who shares our history if not us? *(Out front)* I have three daughters. *(Beat)* King Lear had three daughters. They think up things you'd have to stand on your head to think up. Like when Emily married the drummer from Arkansas in June and divorced him in January or when Joanna went to live in a monastery in Bhutan to find her center, and ended up finding it on Wall Street as a commodities broker. Bo always held to the "Eat your ice cream while it's on your plate," philosophy. *(She exits.)*

EMILY: It's impossible coming home.

BO: It's humiliating; but at the same time, it feels safe.

EMILY: But it doesn't feel *real,* because it's not our real life anymore.

BO: Then what *is*, like our "real" life?

EMILY: That's the thing. It could be *this* life, our *afterlife, one of our previous lives*—I'm certain I was once the Queen of some large country and wore important gold jewelry.

BO: I don't buy that spiritual shit.

EMILY: I believe that spiritual shit.

BO: You've always had trouble facing reality, Em. Like the time you built a tent in the backyard and made believe you were the Jews struggling to cross the desert and all summer we had to bring you out water

EMILY: You've always been judgmental, just like Mother.

BO: Because I have values.

EMILY: *(Sarcastically)* Unlike valueless me.

BO: You just like to shock. Come on, taking up with a sultan from Bali.

EMILY: Objection. Titi is not from Bali. He was born in the Bronx and his name is Arnold Mitterman.

BO: But he's *still* a sultan and that's weird. I mean how did he get from the Bronx to Sultanhood?

EMILY: If you promise not to talk about it when he gets here.

BO: He's coming HERE?

EMILY: End of the week. I didn't tell Mom yet. He's trying to get a cheap flight.

BO: I thought he was a sultan.

EMILY: He *is*, but he's a *poor* sultan. And he got to be a Sultan because he was involved with the son of the King of Sumba, Emerald Star. Emerald owned three sultanates and gave one to Arnold. Now they've broken up, but Arnold is still technically a Sultan. *(Beat)* Okay, so he's bi-sexual, but he's totally in love with *me* now, and that's what counts. And yes, our sex is normal; in fact, off the map.

(There is silence.)

BO: What's Mother going to say?

EMILY: I told her Arnold inherited his title from a distant relative.

BO: She's not that stupid.

EMILY: Parents can be very stupid when they don't want to know the truth.

BO: She's a mature, *New York* woman, Emily. She can take ANYTHING. *(Beat)* You think she's really going this time?

EMILY: Come on. She's been saying that for years. When we were growing up it was her biggest threat. "You kids keep this up and I'm leaving you at the super market and moving to Paris."

BO: No. This time she's serious. She has a renter, she's packing, AND she's turning sixty. They say it's the MOST dangerous birthday.

(GARY enters, papers in hand.)

GARY: Emily, how goes your amoebae?

EMILY: Multiplying, thank you.

GARY: Okay, ladies, let's go! Closed book quiz. Texas. Best milk shake?

BO: Avalon's Drug Store in Houston.

GARY: Best hamburger in Texas?

BO: Blue Mesa Grill in Dallas.

GARY: Top seafood?

BO: Captain Benny's?

GARY: Pork ribs?

BO: City Market in Luling, made on the pitmaster. *(To* EMILY*)* He grades me. It makes me so nervous.

EMILY: *(As she exits)* Don't you two think of anything else but food?

BO: Sometimes, but we wipe it right out of our minds.

GARY: *(To* BO*)* About the menu for the dinner, Bo, I thought our maha*gonny* fried chicken. *(Pronounced with a long "o")*

BO: You mean "ma*hog*any". Ma-ha-*gonny* is a Kurt Weill opera. And this is just an observation, but have

you noticed when you make *your* fried chicken, there
are always leftovers?

GARY: Because it's so satisfying.

BO: Because it's so heavy.

GARY: What would you suggest?

(Beat)

BO: *(Beat)* Can't we just love each other?

*(GARY and BO exit as VI enters, sits at her desk, and turns
on the computer to an interactive C D program to learn
French. The pictures of the objects come onto the screen)*

VOICE FROM COMPUTER: Repeat after me. *Repetez
aprez-moi. Le lémon.*

VI: *Le lemon.*

VOICE FROM COMPUTER: *Non. (Then repeating) Le lémon.*

VI: *Le lemon.*

VOICE FROM COMPUTER: *Non. Repetez s'il vous plais. Le
lémon.*

VI: Okay. *(Takes a deep breath) Le lémon.*

VOICE FROM COMPUTER: *Excellent. Continuez.... La
baguette. Avez-vouz* une *baguette?*

VI: *Avez-vous* une *(een) baguette.*

VOICE FROM COMPUTER: *(Correcting her) Une. (Oon)..Une
(Oon), Une (Oon)!*

VI: Une.

VOICE FROM COMPUTER: Bravo.

*(JOANNA enters carrying a briefcase and overnight bag. She
is in Brooks Brothers classic)*

JOANNA: Sorry. The Jersey Turnpike was backed up
half way to Philadelphia.... It's airless in here.

VI: Where's Phil?

JOANNA: In Maine.

VI: What is he doing in Maine? He's supposed to be here. I knew I should have written his parents directly and say " La dee da, etcetera." Do they know what time dinner is?

JOANNA: They're not coming.

VI: What do you mean they're not coming? Of course they're coming.

JOANNA: They're *not coming*.

VI: How can we plan the wedding if they're not coming?

JOANNA: There's no wedding. It's off.

VI: It's just nerves. Your father got hiccoughs before our wedding and we had to put a paper bag over his head... Look, I've ordered one hundred and twenty gold chairs and grilled baby salmon..

JOANNA: Phyl ran off with Monica, a soprano from the Metropolitan opera, and incidentally, one of my best friends.

VI: I don't believe it.

JOANNA: Believe it. Phyl went to Maine and I was beside myself thinking it was depression.

VI: But there are drugs. It's nothing to be ashamed of. Half the people I know are walking around medicated.

JOANNA: I thought Phyl went to Maine to jump off a cliff; but it turned out Phyl was hardly depressed and, in fact, was fucking Monica's brains out in the Holiday Inn at Bar Harbor.

VI: *(Trying to hug her.* JOANNA *is stiff)*

Poor baby. I hate men. Do you see women running around sowing their wild oats over every open meadow?

JOANNA: *(Breaking away)* Phyl is a woman, Ma. I know this is inexcusable to wait till the last minute to tell you, but I was afraid of your reaction. *(Silence)* I know you're "hip", but underneath beats the heart of a bourgeois. It's not your fault. It's genetic. *(Beat)* Well I'm gay. I have been for years...as in lesbian. You know all those woman teachers I had crushes on, the tennis players, cousin Eleanor...

VI: *(Interrupting)* Cousin Eleanor! What did you do with Cousin Eleanor? Oh my God, Club Med! You went to Club Med with Cousin Eleanor! She's not ...?

JOANNA: She *is*.

VI: You did it with your own cousin?

JOANNA: We didn't *do* it. We just hung out.

VI: But the wedding… You must take me for a fool. This Phil was coming with his parents, I mean *her* parents. What about her parents?

JOANNA: They've had us for dinner. They're lovely.

VI: You've completely shut me out, Joanna.

JOANNA: All you think about is yourself. *I've been jilted.*

VI: And you let me go ahead and order the wedding cake with a little bride and a groom on it.

JOANNA: I was going to tell you.

VI: When? I had my wedding dress cleaned for you! *(She runs to the closet, takes out a wedding dress wrapped in plastic, thrusting at JOANNA)* Here! You said you wanted to wear it.

JOANNA: *(Holding the dress)* I *planned* to wear it.

VI: And what about Phil?

JOANNA: She planned to wear her grandmother's wedding dress. Her grandmother's descended from the Mayflower.

VI: How American. And both your sisters knew.

(JOANNA *nods her head.*)

VI: Everyone knew except dopo here. Have they met Phyl? Well not Emily, of course. Emily's always somewhere else.

JOANNA: Emily's studying foreign cultures. She <u>has</u> to be somewhere else. And yes, Bo and Gary met Phyllis. They said it was like having another sister.

VI: But what do we give a damn about Phyllis now anyway, seeing she ran off with Monica.

JOANNA: It's not a joke. I'm asking you for acceptance.

VI: I'm sorry. I'm in shock. Not about you being gay, I mean. Okay. Maybe a little. But my naievete...

JOANNA: *You! You! You!*

VI: So *you you you*! The wedding, everything... everything turning…turning fifty. And I'm not common and bourgeois.

JOANNA: Of course you aren't ..totally. If you were, how could you produce US?

(JOANNA *and* VI *simultaneously, next two speeches*)

JOANNA: We just put a deposit on a Lexus together and were going to the Greek Islands for our honeymoon. *(Beat)* I bought a white string bikini.

VI: *(Simultaneously with previous speech)* I do what I do because I *want* to. Months ago I rented a house. I looked at pictures, saw this one, pointed to it, and said "That's the one I want". It had a blue door and a window seat. *(Beat)* I'm sad for you, Joanna. Honest. It's a terrific disappointment. *(She tries to hug* JOANNA *who is still holding the billowing wedding dress, so she is hard to get near.)* Bo's a mess, I know. And Emily's a bacterial disaster, but I'm still going… I *am*... *(Beat)* …. devastated.

JOANNA: Well so am I. *(Beat)* And Phyllis did not go graciously into the night. I left for work like any morning—showered, ran for the train. After work I went to the gym. When I got home, I rang the doorbell, which I do because Phyllis gets home first, and it's such a bitch to put your briefcase down, and the groceries , and search through your bag for the key. No one answered, so I unlocked the door. *(Beat)* The apartment was emptied out.

VI: The big screen T V? Everything?

JOANNA: Just the stuff that was hers, which was *almost* everything. She drove up in a truck after I left for work. My doorman told me she and Monica cleaned the place out in a heartbeat. I miss the ping-pong table which we used as a dining room table... It's easy to understand what you like to do when you're suddenly not doing it anymore. *(She exits, near tears.)*

VI: *(Out front)* It was at this moment something in me knew this was the last of the good days, of this brownstone as I knew it, these rooms. And by the end of the summer I would close the door and go to a new place and never be able to get back here to the time when I thought everything would turn out the way I wanted.

GARY: *(Entering barefoot, herbs in hand)* Fried chicken's all wrong. It's too hot out. I've decided on a southwestern salad—cold corn, salsa, beans and cilantro. Cilantro's the key.

VI: Have you lost your mind? How can we serve cold beans for an engagement dinner, even if we aren't having one? A formal dinner is hot unless you're living in Ecuador. And how come no one told me about Joanna?

GARY: *(Picking up cilantro)* But Jesus, just *smell* this cilantro! *(Putting it up to* VI's *nose)*

VI: I don't want to smell the cilantro, Gary, and there *is no engagement dinner*. Joanna's gay. Oh, but you knew that. Only now she's been jilted and I don't know what in the hell's going on here. Emily's parasitic, and you and Bo are like a pair of Canada geese, dropping stuff all over the place. I don't understand. You all started out as *normal* people. You and Barbara had a *normal* wedding, a regular childhood, piano lessons, "Curious George". This is not the sixties. You're not hippies. How do you come up with cold beans?

GARY: *(Slowly, formally, in a huff)* Would you rather the chicken, Viola?

VI: Yes I would, fried chicken, swimming in gravy. Gary, Gary, whatl happened to my girls?

GARY: They left home.

VI: If they left, how come they're all back? Don't answer. Look, all of you can't stay. I need to go. I'm like *The Three Sisters* trying to get to Moscow. We don't know if they got there, whether life would be any different for them. But they *think* it would. That's the thing. *(Beat)* Have I ever said "No" if it's important? It's not like any of you are homeless.

GARY: *(To VI)* To be *brutally honest*...

VI: *(Breaking in)* I shudder when someone says that to me?

GARY: Bo needs you.

VI: Barbara's not easy, Gary. She's an Aquarius. They're complicated.

GARY: She cries all the time.

VI: She's unhappy.

GARY: She doesn't like sex anymore.

VI: It's probably all that food she's filling up on.

GARY: She doesn't find me attractive. That's what she said.

VI: You're very attractive, Gary. And now *I'll* be brutally honest. Are you having an affair?

GARY: How would I have the time?

VI: If the President of the United States had time, anyone has time. You didn't answer me.

GARY: We'll be finished with the book in a week, Vi, and that's it. Our lease is up in Berkeley and I'll move in with a buddy.

VI: And there is no renovation going on , is there.

GARY: *(Shaking his head in agreement)* Maybe Bo could go to France with you. You know you. You'd get lonely in a couple of days. And you hardly speak the language. Bo's fluent. And she'd cook for you.

VI: She can't come with me.

GARY: What Bo said is she doesn't want to *sleep* with me, but she wants to *be* with me; I don't turn her on, but she's afraid to be alone.

*(*BO *enters, in a panic)*

VI: What's the matter?

BO: *(To* VI*)* I just had a panic attack at Zabar's, right in front of the deli counter. Eight varieties of lox. How are you supposed to choose? Irish, Scottish, smoked or dilled! God! Is there any way you can leave later? I mean, I'd have to go to California and get my stuff. Then I'd come back.

GARY: *(To* BO*)* I suggested you go to France *with* your mother. It would be good for you. Wild mushrooms, fresh pate...

BO: *(To* GARY*)* How do you know what's good for me?

GARY: Well I did think *I* was good for you..

(EMILY *enters, red-eyed.*)

EMILY: I've been throwing up my guts for a solid hour.

VI: Then call the Doctor.

EMILY: I did. It's not the amoeba. Well I did have an amoeba, its true, but it seems... (*Wiping her eyes, then clinking a knife against a glass*) It seems in addition to the amoeba, which is now cured, Doctor Hill said ... I'm in my first trimester.

(*Long silence, then*)

GARY: Well honey, that's beautiful.

EMILY: Okay, I'm saying the word...pregnant. They did the test. I'm going to be a Mom!.

VI: Is it okay to ask who the father of the baby is?

EMILY: Titi, of course.

GARY: Who's Titi?

VI: Arnold.

BO: The sultan.

EMILY: I wonder if that would make the baby a princess or a prince? Prince Mitterman of Bali. (*Beat*) It's scary. How am I supposed to teach now? My whole life is going down the toilet. (*To* VI) But it's going to be okay because Titi's coming. That's the good part. He's coming, any minute…
I just hadn't exactly told you yet.

VI: Coming where?

BO: Here.

EMILY: Here.

VI: If I'm such an intelligent woman, why am I the last to learn anything?
    What else don't I know? Come on. Lay it on the table, girls. My cup runneth over. (*Pouring herself a scotch*)

BO: We don't tell you some stuff till it's over, because sometimes you can't handle it.

VI: That's because I am still processing the "stuff" you told me before.

GARY: If you'll excuse me, I'll see to dinner. Is it okay if I use the bottle of Mouton '87 I spied in the cabinet? It <u>is</u> a celebration. You're going to be a Mommy, Emily.

(EMILY starts to cry)

GARY: *(To* BO*)* And you're going to be an aunt, Bo.

(BO starts to cry.)

EMILY: *(To* VI*)* And you, Mom, are going to be a Grandma.

(VI starts to weep. EMILY joins in. GARY exits. Three women are crying when JOANNA enters , dark glasses on. She looks at all three of them, doesn't say a word, then starts to cry)

VI: I know. *(Out front)* Little did I know that I didn't know the half of it. " This new news was announced like "Your sofa will be delivered on Friday".... The next evening we gathered around the table to enjoy the non-engagement dinner, anticipating the arrival of the sultan.

(VI, BO, JOANNA and GARY enter and seat themselves around the table. They eat in absolute silence. There is south-western salad, platters of fried chicken, and wine. VI shovels in piece after piece of fried chicken, picking it up, cleaning it to the bone. GARY, a napkin tucked into his shirt, eats everything, slowly, and with deep sighs of appreciation. BO picks. JOANNA eats nothing.)

VI: Great beans.

JOANNA: Well I think it's wonderful about Emily. Phyllis and I were planning a turkey baster child.

VI: And I don't see why the sultan can't take a cab from the airport, why Emily has to drive out to Kennedy, in her condition. He should have hired a limo. My God, he's a sultan.

GARY: Maybe they wanted to be alone.

BO: She needs to tell him she's...you know...

VI: I think I should call your father. Pass the chicken, please.

BO: He's in Florida.

VI: He couldn't. He hates Florida, the way the lounge chairs are lined up in straight rows around the swimming pools, waiting for the Messiah.

JOANNA: They went to a spa.

VI: He and the skin doctor...

JOANNA: The dermatologist, He's trying to get his body back in shape.

VI: The man's reinventing himself. Someone saw him riding a Harley in a leather jacket.

Still, I should call. We have some developments here and he deserves to know. For starters, there's no wedding. *(To* JOANNA*)* I'm sorry, honey. And *Phil* is *Phyllis.* Oh, I forgot. Your father met her so he knows that Phil is Phyllis.

JOANNA: Please do *not* mention her name again in my presence. And I'll deal with Daddy.

VI: But Emily's expecting our first grandchild, and I want to share that with him. *Wait a minute!* Maybe *Emily* will get married. Then we won't have to cancel the caterer after all.

JOANNA: *(To* VI*)* This is just what I'm talking about. You're too hung up on traditional values.. You know, a lot of people are getting married on their child's first birthday. One couple I know served caviar and teething bagels.

GARY: Look at *us. We* married.

VI: That too. I have to tell your father about you and Bo splitting.

BO: This is one great call to get at a spa.

VI: Why should I be the only one enjoying these cultural events?

JOANNA: We'll tell him *after* his vacation.

VI: Oh by all means, don't spoil his vacation. *(Beat.To* BO) Maybe you could stay with *him* when he gets back.

BO: That is the stupidest idea! I'm comfortable here! You know, some kids don't even want to come home. But *we* do..

JOANNA: Because we love you.

VI: So if you do...let me go.

JOANNA: *(To* VI) Who's holding you prisoner?

VI: *(Out front)* The answer to that question eluded me, but I knew *if* I knew it, it would be the key to many of the mysteries of the universe.

GARY: *(To* JOANNA) What was the menu for the wedding, Joanna? I'm curious. *(No response)* It's a perfectly professional question.

JOANNA: Grilled salmon.

VI: *(Adding) Baby charred* salmon.

JOANNA: *(To* GARY) Parsleyed potatoes, and asparagus bundles tied with red pimento, and thank you for asking. *(She bolts from the room.)*

BO: *(To* GARY) *Now* look what you've done.

GARY: Sue me because I have an *appetite for life.*

VI: Which appears to be an occupational hazard with this family.

(EMILY *bursts into the room with* ARNOLD *and his luggage. He is wearing a Batik shirt, shorts, sandals, has a pony tail.*)

EMILY: We're home! EVERYONE, *THIS* IS ARNOLD!

VI: *(To* ARNOLD, *shaking his hand)* I'm Emily's mother. *(Beat)* What a relief. I thought you'd be wearing a turban.

ARNOLD: Actually, I used to wear rings on my toes, but it was hard walking. *(Pressing his palms together in front of him, Indonesian greeting)* Selamat malam. Good evening.

EMILY: My sister Bo, her husband, Gary. Where's Joanna?

VI: Crying in the bathroom. *(To* ARNOLD*)* It's been a zoo of a week. Shall I call you Arnold or Sultan?

EMILY: Arnold's Sumbanese name is Titi. *(Beat)* Excuse me. I feel another wave of nausea coming on. *(She exits.)*

VI: She's having morning sickness at night, same as I did. *(Beat)* Look, Arnold, hello and let me be straight with you.

ARNOLD: You want us to get married.

VI: You got it.

ARNOLD: You probably want to meet my parents too, but you can't.

VI: I can't.

ARNOLD: They've disowned me because of my relationship with Emerald Star.

VI: Who's Emerald Star?

ARNOLD: *The son* of the *King* of *Sumba—my friend* when I was, you know...

VI: No, I didn't know.

BO: *(To* ARNOLD*)* Do you plan to get married?

GARY: *(To* BO*)* That's rude, Bo!

BO: I'm curious. *(To* ARNOLD*) Do* you?

VI: *(TO* ARNOLD*)* Please excuse Bo. She's distraught because she's splitting with her husband. My other daughter, whom you haven't met yet, is gay, and her impending marriage has just been...what's the word - cancelled. *(Beat)* Mister Arnold, Sultan Titi, your timing is such that you've landed yourself on the other side of the moon here.

ARNOLD: Emily and I believe in prudence. *(Beat, then "prudence" in Indonesian) Hati-hati.*

VI: *(To* ARNOLD*)* Mister Mitterman—god you have a lot of names. It's confusing. I only know you're from the Bronx, you went to Bali, and you have now impregnated my daughter.

ARNOLD: *That word* scares the shit out of me.

VI: Well it scares the shit out of me too, but it's better than "fucked". *(Beat)* Look, everyone, you have all come home visiting more plagues on me than Pharoah visited on the Israelites... Not that a new life on earth is a plague. It's a blessing. *However,* at the moment, I do not feel, may I say, especially "blessed".

(Spot up on EMILY *with* JOANNA*)*

GARY: *(To* ARNOLD*)* Sultan, this is Joanna. Joanna, the Sultan.

JOANNA: And I'm the gay one. Congratulations. We wish you every heterosexual happiness.

ARNOLD: *(To* JOANNA*)* Emily told me what happened. I'm sure you'll meet someone else.

VI: *(To* JOANNA*)* Or you could change your mind and broaden your horizons.

JOANNA: The parental fantasy, the wayward daughter comes to her senses about her sexual identity.

VI: A friend's son did. He went to a hypnotist. Lennie Rubenstein.

JOANNA: Lennie Rubenstein's an asshole.

VI: Lennie Rubenstein's a full Professor at Columbia.

JOANNA: He's still an asshole.

ARNOLD: We, however, are menches and want to assure you we plan to go ahead with this child. I know it's crazy we had to go to Bali to meet each other, and you all must be "concerned" regarding my recent past, but that's why it's called "past". (To VI) And yo, what if I was *your* kid? Wouldn't you pray I'd straighten out? You don't know the half of it.

EMILY: (To ARNOLD) You should probably spare my mother that part.

VI: Oh, come on. Lay it on me. I have the hide of a hyena.

And can I ask how a nice Jewish boy like you ended up in the middle of the South Pacific?

ARNOLD: The call of the exotic. As a young boy I wanted to be the bearded lady in the circus, which was pretty confusing.

(As the tale unfolds, everyone starts to cut into the pie, down to scraping the bottom off the pie plate, swirling their fingers around for the last bits of peach)

ARNOLD: Then I fell in love with Judy Garland in *The Wizard Of Oz*. I wanted red shoes like Dorothy, which kind of threw me off. So I went to PayLess and got some red high heel pumps. My mother discovered them under my bed about the same time I discovered Christopher Davis. He liked Judy Garland too. One thing led to another and when my parents found out, they sent me straight to Teresa Mae Mullins, a therapist who tried mightily to swing me around. That went on for a year, until graduation, screwing in her reclining chair four o'clock every Monday afternoon. It was then I realized, and to her credit, that I was a switch hitter. So that should reassure all of you of my abiding love for Emily, —that I *can*, if you know what I mean, love her.

(There is a stunned silence.)

EMILY: *(Taking* ARNOLD*'s hand)* Arnold and I decided on the way back from the airport; we're not returning to Bali.

ARNOLD: The economy's too unstable there.

EMILY: We want to be near family. We feel a strong need to nest.

VI: And you'll be nesting *where*?

EMILY: *(To* VI*)* We'd go to Westchester, but Arnold and his parents aren't speaking because of his bi-sexuality. The King of Sumba period.

VI: *(Out front)* About now I was getting one of my major migraines, like if they told me one more thing my head was going to fall off:, also, it was good, my mother wasn't alive, because then I'd have to explain all of this to her and let's not even go there. *(Turning back to the table)* I've been dreaming about this summer for years *(Beat)* And there are other people involved.

GARY: *(To* BO, *who is now ravenously reaching for the chicken, gobbling it)* If you want, we could go back to Berkeley, sign the lease for another year, and live dysfunctionally in our house.

JOANNA: I'd offer my apartment, but it's in the middle of New Jersey and it's tinsy. *(Nodding towards* VI*)* Clearly, she'd cancel the rental, but she needs the money to pay for the French thing.

VI: Please don't refer to me as "she" when I'm in the room.

EMILY: *(To VI)* Nothing's going to stop you from getting what you want this time, is it?.

VI: *This time, nothing will.*

JOANNA: You *could* tell the renter the truth.

BO: That we returned unexpectedly.

(During all of this VI is silent.)

JOANNA: *(To her sisters)* Then I could come over after work, and it would be like old times, all of us together, like some dreary family in a sad Chekhov play.

VI: It's not going to work this time, wearing me down. I have my heart set.

EMILY: Well I didn't have one piece of my heart set on having this baby right now!

VI: *(Out front)* Of course it *was working*. My choices were "rotten mother of the year" or "failed novelist". At that moment I saw a cruise ship steaming down the Hudson, and on the decks, I pictured passengers having their first martini of the day while the band warmed up in the ballroom, and I tell you, I wanted to be on that ship… *(Then, gently, turning back To EMILY)* You'll manage, Emily, you'll see. Then you won't be able to imagine your life without a child. *(Giving EMILY a kiss on the cheek)* You'll *all* triumph over your adversities.

EMILY: Spare us the "it will make us stronger" thing.

VI: It won't. That's just a saying mothers invented. After dinner drinks? *(Then out front)* Every summer I'd gone to London. I was mad for London. My ex could take or leave London. He could take or leave most anything. He'd stay for a week, then he'd go. Then, I'd rent a car, and drive through the countryside, drive

as though my life depended on it. I loved the little
cathedral towns to the south—Salisbury, Winchester...
Winchester Cathedral... *(Singing the first line)*
"Winchester Cathedral, you're bringing me down..."
*(Trailing off, humming second bar of song, going to the
liquor cabinet)*

(Lights up on ARNOLD*)*

ARNOLD: Westchester, where my family moved to in
our post-Bronx period, was pretty normal. The usual
good schools, drugs, great bagels. Adolescence was no
picnic. I used to feel this pecking inside me, something
wanting to get out. After graduation, I planned to go
to college and study with Tobias Wolfe who also had a
tortured childhood. Instead, I took out this globe, spun
it, and my finger went straight to Indonesia, the largest
archipelago in the world. So I went to Bali to study
fabrics. My father's in the garment business, so it made
perfect sense. *(Beat)* It's been a long day. I'm going to
say goodnight, Selamat tidur.

VI: *(To* ARNOLD *as he exits)* Titi, when you're bi-sexual
does that mean you can change back at any moment, or
that whatever you are *now* is not what you *used* to be?
And you can use the small bedroom upstairs, on the
left.

ARNOLD: *(As he exits)* Thank you and that's the thing.
You never know. But, I'll say this: whatever side of the
plate you're hitting from, you're happy.

GARY: If you'll excuse me, maybe you women want
to be alone. I'm going out to look at the moon. I hear
there's a man in it. *(He exits.)*

EMILY: What do you think?

JOANNA: About what?

EMILY: Him?

VI: Do you love him?

EMILY: It's hard to know anything when you're nauseous.

VI: I asked if you love him?

EMILY: I'm twenty-eight, and whether I met him under a palm tree or in a field of snow, he'd be the one. He would find me up the Amazon, I would discover him at the top of Notre Dame. *(Beat)* He wrote my name in orchids on the beach, fastened them to the sand with chop sticks... Isn't it mad how we had to go half way around the world to meet?

JOANNA: No. It's beautiful. I'm envious. What I wonder is how could *some* of us *end up* so *fucked up*?

BO: I think I'll turn gay like Joanna.

JOANNA: You don't "turn" gay. You just are. And you'd know if you were. You'd want to kiss a woman.

(BO shakes her head.)

JOANNA: *(To BO)* Then you're not.

VI: Look, I feel awful saying this, but for some of us, the older you get, the farther you get from your luck, so... I'm not going to France just to write a novel. I've met someone and I'm meeting him there.

BO: Not Larry!

VI: God, no. The man fell asleep at the opera, just when Aida was about to swallow the poison. *(Beat)* His name is Avery. We met at a party. We're taking it slowly.

BO: She's saying she didn't sleep with him *yet.*

VI: Avery just happened. At the time I wasn't looking. People can walk in when you don't even know the door's open. He makes documentary films. It could have been his sound. Avery has a voice like velvet. He says to me, "Do you wow everyone?" "Not everyone," I say, "just selectively." I didn't know I wowed anything. I felt fifteen years old again. *(Silence)* He was married, but a long time ago.

EMILY: That's *very* suspicious, Mom, a fabulous guy who's single. Is he ugly or are you sure he's straight?

VI: He's *very* attractive, and, yes, he likes women. Well we kissed. We don't know each other *that* well.

BO: *(To VI)* Then what do you want to do with a perfect stranger all summer in France?

JOANNA: We can only guess.

VI: Joanna! Come on. It's for companionship.

BO: If it was for companionship then I could come. And *I cook.* Does *he* cook?

EMILY: This friend of Mom's is too busy doing *other* things.

VI: Okay. So we've slept with each other.

JOANNA: Was he good in bed?

BO: If he didn't want a turkey sandwich after you made love, he's good.

EMILY: Not true. We always eat afterwards.

JOANNA: We do it *during.*

VI: *(To EMILY)* Do you know I love you?

EMILY: Yes.

VI: *(To BO)* Do you know I love *you*?

BO: Most of the time.

VI: *(To JOANNA)* Do you know I love you?

JOANNA: When I do what you want me to, you do.

VI: Avery is in town. He's parked across the street waiting till you go to sleep. Would you like to meet him?

JOANNA: The man is outside in his car waiting like some teenager? Tell him to come in!

BO: But what about the house. Us staying? We could pay the rent. I could take out a loan. Emily could sell her semi-precious jewelry.

VI: I don't know. We'll see.

EMILY: When we were little and you said that it meant...

JOANNA: No.

VI: We'll see.

(VI *flashes the outdoor light to signal* AVERY, *then leaves to go out to the front landing…as she's walking*)

Since you're no longer little and helpless, and I'm older and more desperate, that's a promise this time.

JOANNA: (*To her sisters*) She'll give in. Guilt is the answer.

(VI *enters with* AVERY. AVERY *is big, black, and beautiful*)

VI: Girls, I'd like you to meet Avery.

EMILY: Holy shit!

(*Lights fade*)

END OF ACT ONE

ACT TWO

(Time: one week later)

(Place: Brownstone. Early Evening. It is unusually serene for this household. All the boxes have been packed away. Sound of Grover Washington's All My Tomorrows. *AVERY and VI dance, real tight and slow. Let them dance for a minute. Don't rush it. Then VI breaks away)*

VI *(Out front)* A week later I was certain the "all the you know what" had now finished hitting the "you know what". *(She shakes her head.)* But I was wrong. It was just getting rolling.

(VI walks back to rejoin AVERY and they dance. Following conversation is above last part of music)

AVERY: I was in Paris once, overnight.

VI: Just overnight.

AVERY: Business.

VI: No one goes to Paris *only* on business.

AVERY: True. I had a great meal.

VI: What else don't I know about you?

AVERY: I'm younger than you.

VI: How younger?

AVERY: Depends how old you are.

VI: Next.

AVERY: I was born in Atlanta.

VI: I know that.

AVERY: Too much talk. Let's just dance.

(They start to dance)

VI: You have two boys.

AVERY: Nelson and Chip.

VI: You'll fall in love with Provence.

AVERY: I've been there and you're right.

VI: I thought you were never there before.

AVERY: Just overnight.

VI: Like Paris.

AVERY: In France we'll live on goose liver and wine. We'll drink ourselves under the table.

VI: What part of Provence, overnight?

AVERY: Marseilles.

VI: Marseilles doesn't count. It's not really Provence.

AVERY: That's what I meant. I've never really been there.

VI: Fair warning. I intend to work.

AVERY: Fair warning. I may have to leave for a couple of weeks. Just to London.

(VI stops dancing. Fade out music.)

AVERY: On assignment. We're doing a piece on the Norfolk Broads.

VI: The women.

AVERY: The flatlands of England.

VI: *(Slowly, as in taking it in)* Really.

AVERY: Canals, swans and windmills, all very British and terribly quaint.

VI: I could come with you.

AVERY: Whoa. You said yourself you have your own work.

VI: The novel. Good God... *(Mockingly slapping one side of her face)* You unnerve me so, I almost forgot.

AVERY: *Focus*, woman. Sex uses up a lot of creative energy. Good that I may have to leave.

VI: Because of work.

AVERY: Because of work.

VI: It's no big deal. It's just a summer in Europe. Let's not make a drama out of it.

AVERY: You got it.

VI: *(Out front)* Of course I didn't have it at all, but nonchalance, ever, in the face of desperation. *(Turning back to* AVERY*)* ...So how come you never remarried?

AVERY: Did I say that?

VI: You said you live alone.

AVERY: That's right.

VI: Well how many times were you married?

AVERY: I see we're having a grilling.

VI: Think of it more as a cook out.

AVERY: Twice.

VI: But just overnight.

AVERY: *(Ticked off)* You want me to leave?

VI: That wasn't nice. I'm sorry.

AVERY: Damn right.

VI: I'm trying not to get invested.

AVERY: The same.

VI: At least we're not at cross purposes.

AVERY: You want to wiggle out? Now's your chance. I'm giving you wiggle room.

VI: Wiggle out of *what*?

AVERY: Exactly.

VI: But I'll bet you've had a gaggle of girlfriends.

AVERY: Oh, yeah.. A battalion of babes.

VI: *(Out front)* You know how sometimes you know they're lying or you're stupid, but you're going to ignore it and choose the "you're just stupid" option because you want things to be the way you want them. But you had to admit he was quick. *(Back to* AVERY*)* And you should know I married the first man I dated in college and that was it.

AVERY: You're talking sex.

VI: I'm talking sex.

AVERY: Do you have a cigarette?

VI: I didn't think you smoked.

AVERY: I don't, but I'm getting nervous.

(VI gets cigarettes. They light up.)

VI: When I was married I was straight as an arrow. Boy, I feel dizzy. I have to sit down. *(She does.)* You know how to make a martini?

AVERY: *(Sarcastically joking)* Just mint juleps. *(Beat)* Vermouth and gin. *(He exits to kitchen.)*

VI: *(Calling after* AVERY*)* And don't forget the olives. *(Speaking louder so* AVERY *can hear)*

Look, Avery, I'm out of my league here. I mean I didn't even know there *was* a G spot until recently.

AVERY: *(From the kitchen).* So I have more experience than you.

VI: *(Not clear if he hears her)* I don't know if I'm being too forward or not forward enough. If I make the wrong move, you could get scared and leave. *(More to herself)* When I come home, sometimes I open the windows just to let some noise in. You'd think I'd be noise enough for myself.

(AVERY enters with martinis.)

AVERY: *(Clinking her glass)* You'd think...Viola...I like to say your whole name...V-I-O-LA.

VI: *(Clinking his glass back)* A-VE-RY...like a kind of sanctuary filled with wild birds—golden plovers, glossy Ibises; they're indigenous to southern France. I bought new binoculars... What do you think of a mother who abandons her kids?

AVERY: Thirty, twenty-eight, twenty-six year old *kids*?

VI: You'd think they'd have it together by now.

AVERY: Like we did. What were *you* doing at that age?

VI: Banning the bomb, growing hair on my legs—it was this big feminist thing then.

AVERY: And where was I? Name one march I wasn't in, a protest I wasn't arrested at. Was I at Watts summer of '65? You bet. Smoking pot? You bet. And I *did* inhale. Probably inhaled the entire damn state of Georgia. *(Beat)* You know you're one of the sexiest women I've ever met.

VI: I am?

AVERY: When are the kids coming back?

VI: We have an hour.

AVERY: That's a lot of pressure for me. I like to go nice and slow. I told you.

VI: ...Do you think I'm pretty?

AVERY: I just told you.

VI: You said "sexy". It's not the same as pretty.

AVERY: Could you not talk so much and just be.

(VI *does, then is about to speak*)

AVERY: Shhh.

(AVERY *places two fingers over* VI's *lips. After a moment*)

VI: Avery...

AVERY: What?

VI: I should just give them the apartment and go.

AVERY: (*Caressing her*) I wouldn't.

VI: Why wouldn't you?

AVERY: Wouldn't I *what*?

VI: Let them have the apartment.

AVERY: It doesn't matter what I would do. You aren't me.

VI: But if I *was* you, why wouldn't I?

AVERY: (*Caressing her*) Boundaries. (*Beat*) Look, do you want to make love or not?

VI: Yes.

AVERY: (*Caressing her back*) Uh huh.

(*Taking time between speeches*)

VI: Uh huh...I like the smell of your body. I love your black, how it looks against my white.

AVERY: (*Kissing her forehead, then moving downward*) From Canada...all the way down south to Mexico...I could ride you all night like an Arabian stallion.

VI: Avery...

AVERY: Uh huh?

VI: I *do* have boundaries. But for God's sake, Emily's pregnant. Am I supposed to throw them out?

AVERY: Yes. You've made plans.

VI: But what would you think, *hypothetically*, if I cancelled the trip?

AVERY: Hypothetically, that I never met a strong woman so afraid of independence.
It builds character for kids to want. To desire. Come on. Let your chicks fly. Come on.

VI: If we stayed in the city, we could still do things like go to museums. Make it like a vacation. We'd drink expensive wines at darling French bistros, hang out at Starbucks… *(Beat)* You'd hate me, wouldn't you. You already bought your plane tickets.

AVERY: I could change them. I can always use a ticket to France.

VI: I don't want my heart cracked. I told you.

AVERY: Hey, don't lay all that power on me. I'm cool either way. You're the one who rented the house.

VI: I think about desire, Avery, *(Beat)* This is embarrassing. *(Beat)* You turn me on.

AVERY: That's not embarrassing. You turn me on too.

VI: If we don't go we'll lose our momentum, and if I stay I'll get sucked in. *(Beat)* I'm a mess, Avery. I'm incapable of making a decision. That's the first sign of a breakdown.

AVERY: I'm not saying *anything.*

(Doorbell)

VI: Good, God! It's Joanna! We have no clothes on. What is she going to think?

(A scramble to get dressed, put back together)

AVERY: That her mother still fucks.

JOANNA: *(Calling out as she enters)* It's okay. I found my keys. It's a steambath out there! Well, I did it! *(Seeing what she's come into)* Oh...excuse me.

VI: *(Rapidly finishing dressing)* I thought you were going to a movie.

JOANNA: It was sold out. Stupid because I heard it was a stupid movie. People are desperate in this city.

VI: It may look it, but we weren't doing anything.

JOANNA: Well I certainly hope you *were*. At least someone in the family's getting it. Guess who I talked to? Arnold's parents! The Mittermans. I called them and I've arranged a meeting between Arnold and them tomorrow at a neutral point, the White Plains Galleria. Emily's coming too and she's a wreck.

VI: I think it's fabulous. *(to* AVERY*)* Joanna was always the most political.

JOANNA: *(Softer, more vulnerable)* And I called Phyllis. I couldn't stop myself. She wished me a good life and said she was deeply sorry for the unfortunate turn of events. Then she said it would "take time."

VI: That was an idiotic thing to say.

JOANNA: Exactly. When I hung up I thought what a idiotic thing to say. What else is there *except* time?

VI: *(Moving to hug her)* I'm sorry. Come here.

JOANNA: It's just a lousy time. Now I'm saying it, "time". Time, time, time, time, time! Oh shit, Ma!...

(JOANNA *begins to cry.*)

(VI *and* JOANNA *hold each other.*)

AVERY: I should leave.

JOANNA: It's okay. I'm okay.

AVERY: I can't stay anyways. I have an appointment uptown.

VI: *(To* AVERY*)* Because of what I said?

AVERY: Because I have an appointment. I'll be back. *(To* JOANNA*)* Is it hot out there?

JOANNA: Not as hot as it is in here.

VI: *(Out front)* The next afternoon the girls were going through the bookshelves and reviewing where things went wrong in alphabetical order. You can see how the cards were getting stacked against me.

*(*VI *exits.* BO *and* JOANNA *are going through the bookcases)*

BO: It used to be right here. After Dickens.

JOANNA: Who's going to steal your Emily Dickenson from the house? And I think it's so like Mother to date someone her mother would disapprove of.

BO: Grandma's dead.

JOANNA: Once you have a Mother, you're judged, even from the grave...
   Since we left, the place has gone to seed. No one keeps up the alphabetical order. *(Taking out a book)* Look at this. *Madame Bovary* next to *Doctor Zhivago.* I spent a whole summer organizing this system.

BO: That awful summer we rented the house on Fire Island, and we all got poison ivy so bad, we had to come home.

JOANNA: Mother was furious, but Daddy was secretly happy he didn't have to commute anymore.

BO: So then Mother did a list of the ten great classics and makes us read them.

JOANNA: I still don't get why *The Old Man And The Sea* is a classic. So the man goes fishing, catches the fish, and throws the fish back. Lots of fisherman do that.

BO: It's a metaphor.

JOANNA: I *know* that.

BO: Ma was always into *something,* one foot in the
poetry of things, the other marching down the
corridors of major malls, like a general leading us into
battle, even if it killed the troops, looking for the right
bra, the perfect dress. *(Beat) You know* she's going to
give in When she actually has to say "pack your bags
and go" —who could say that to a child?

JOANNA: She never *could* handle seeing us suffer; <u>and</u>
she's probably shaking in her pants to go away with
this guy. You know her. She likes the *idea* of it.

BO: If we convince her to let us stay, it could be like old
times. We could fight over the bathrooms and drink up
all the diet Coke... Who said you can't go home again?

JOANNA: Thomas Wolfe, and *everything's* different. Our
bikes aren't in the downstairs hall anymore, and she
keeps Absolut in the freezer now, instead of Kool-pops.
I think how when we left for college, we really left, like
we went out the door and they changed the locks.

BO: They changed the locks because they were robbed.

JOANNA: I mean metaphorically.

BO: I *know* what you mean.

JOANNA: Did you know Ma was once in love with a
hippie artist, but her parents disapproved. And in
those days you didn't screw if you weren't married.

BO: I don't want to hear this.

JOANNA: Because you never understood why she and
Dad separated.

BO: *(Hands over her ears)* Don't want to hear this.

JOANNA: People split, Bo, because they fall out of love.

BO: Bullshit! You don't fall out of love like you fall out
of a tree.

JOANNA: It was a Sunday night and you were away at camp. First, Dad said something about cemetery plots. Then *Ma said* she was in favor of cremation. She was at the sink draining linguini. One thing led to another, and she walked over to the table, turned the colander upside down, and the linguine came spilling down the side of his face like rain...just like rain. I kept thinking it was a good thing she hadn't put the marinara sauce on yet. No one said anything for what seemed like forever....

After that, Dad took off.

BO: Why'd you tell me that story?

JOANNA: I don't know.

BO: No! So I'd feel bad, so you don't have to feel bad *alone*! You always do that. It's totally passive aggressive.

JOANNA: Isn't it time to drop the competition? We're practically middle- aged women, and you're still paranoid about me.

BO: Like I was paranoid when I accused you of destroying my butterfly collection, and you denied it?

JOANNA: That was twenty years ago and I was four fucking years old.

BO: So you admit it! It took all summer to collect them. Six different species; Zebra, Monarch, Tiger Swallowtail, Tortoise shell, Cabbage, and the Great Spangled Fritilarry. I sat in my room and cried through dinner, and missed prime ribs and mashed potatoes.

JOANNA: I tried putting them together with Elmer's glue. When that didn't work, I threw them in the pond to see if they could swim.

BO: *(to JOANNA)* You drowned my butterflies in the pond?!

JOANNA: That's it! I'm *buying* you a new butterfly collection, straight uptown to the Museum of Natural History?

BO: You don't *buy* a collection. The thrill is in the *hunt, capturing the damn things, swooping down* with your net. You were just pissed I had something you didn't.

JOANNA: I *thought* they could *fly*! I was a kid! How did I know what *dead* was? I apologize.

BO: *(Beat)* Okay.

JOANNA: Okay.

BO: It wasn't your fault. Our family was trained to compete. *(Beat)* ...Hey, if I'm up against it this summer, do you think I could stay at your place.

JOANNA: Grow up and lie a little, Bo. Tell Gary you changed your mind... You don't have to sleep with him; just live with him. *(Beat)* Look. it stinks we're both down the same time, but I can't take anything else on right now. Even *you.* .

BO: Guess what I wrote in my journal last night? "Terrified, terrified, and terrified".

JOANNA: Last night I couldn't sleep, so I named all the women in my life in chronological order.

EMILY: *(Bursting in)* What a day! Everyone was weeping and hugging right in front of the cosmetic counter at Neiman Marcus. Arnold stayed at the Mall to shop with his mother. Then Maury—that's the father —drove me back and said we could stay with them. He said they're quote "swimming in space." Oh, and they have a swimming pool. They forced bagels on us. They claim they're better in Westchester. They claim everything's better in Westchester. Like I have this feeling nothing bad ever happens there, except for that diet doctor who got murdered.

BO: You can't move to Westchester. You said you wanted to stay *here*.

EMILY: So I can change my mind.

BO: And *what* would you do in Westchester? Bake an apple pie?

EMILY: What's wrong with baking pies? **You** do it.

BO: *Correction*. I *eat* them.

EMILY: Face it. We were raised by upwardly mobile parents to be intellectual snobs. We were shoved into non-conformity. The crime was to be *ordinary*. I've always lived my life in opposition to the norm. *(Beat)* When I was in India, on the road from Dakka to Calcutta, the streets were crowded with the smell of monkeys and parrots, buffalo and pigs, together with lawyers,and holy people and streams of beggars. And in the fields, women in saris were carrying baskets of cow dung on their heads. When we stopped to picnic by the water, these same women were emptying their dung into the lake. And overhead, birds were swooping down, and fish were diving for this dung, and we sat there eating our cheese sandwiches, and I thought … *life, sewage, death, life, sewage death, life, sewage, death*. *(Beat)* Lately it's been getting so exhausting, shlepping all over the world trying to be Margaret Mead.

VI: *(Entering dragging a black suitcase on wheels)* Who said Margaret Mead? I adore that woman, running back and forth to Samoa, collecting husbands like postage stamps. *(Rolling the suitcase back and forth)*

Voila! New suitcase. And I was thinking we should have a party tomorrow night before I go, because on my real fiftieth I'll be in France. I mean when will we all be together again in one place? Emily could be in God know's where a year from now.

BO: Westchester.

VI: And Bo *could* be travelling, checking out bouillabaisse, and Joanna....

JOANNA: *(Finishing sentence)*

Could move to Northampton and be on the cutting edge of the American lesbian scene.

VI: *(Turning to* BO*)* I'd love it if you and Gary could cook me a birthday dinner.

BO: The mood Gary's in, he may feed us cyanide.

JOANNA: *(To* VI*)* I don't believe you're going to dump your own kids.

VI: You mean "keep my plans"?

JOANNA: You're our biological mother. You have no choice.

VI: Oh, but I do. I'm making it.

BO: And where are we supposed to go?

VI: Home.

BO: This *is* our home. Home is the place when you come there they have to take you in. Robert Frost said it.

VI: *(Out front)* And with that the real war was on. Did biology imply responsibility? Wasn't my job to make myself obsolete? In Africa , on a safari, I watched how the mothers sent their children on their way in the bush...baby zebras and lions, little rhinos and giraffes... They gave them their tits, then told them to GO! Make your own home! Protect yourself from the leopard hiding in the trees! It's a law of nature.

Okay. Look at Bambi! Her mother dies and she manages. *(Back to* BO*)* You could stay with Joanna.

JOANNA: It's not the right time.

VI: Well it's not the right time for me either. I finally met someone I like, who likes me.

BO: So go off with him if you're so ga-ga, and stay in bed all day, but that will be the end of writing your next novel. All you'll ever write again are shopping lists.

(Dead silence)

VI: You girls can stand on your heads, but I'm going after it.

EMILY: *(To Vi)* Sometimes I wonder if you know who we really are. When I was fourteen you were so naive, Mother. I mean an all A student suddenly flunks everything, and is out of it, and you never get it. I was a pot head!

VI: Thank you, Emily, for that information after all these years.

BO: If you'll excuse me, I have a sudden craving for mallomars.

VI: We haven't stocked mallomars since they were declared junk food.

BO: Then I have a craving for *some*thing. *(She exits.)*

VI: *(Out front. as* BO *exits)* Bo had always been a hungry child. The girl could eat a horse. *(Turning back to* BO *and* JOANNA*)* Look, I thought I was one terrific mother. The birthday with the Hawaiian theme, a hoola hoop for every kid? The Beach Party in February, white sheets spread on the living room floor, real sand brought in from Jones Beach?

JOANNA: But I asked for a cowgirl theme. Kelly Martin said the Beach idea was stupid, and the kids got cold in their bathing suits. Admit your own work isn't enough. You always want to write our lives.

VI: Because I pray for something conventional to happen in this family.

JOANNA: Oh Avery's *very* conventional. Every white girls' middle-aged mom has a black lover.

VI: Black and white is an accepted practice in our society.

JOANNA: For *us*, not for *you*. You're the adult! You let us get away with murder. Emily was doing drugs! Bo was stuffing herself into a stupor! I was running around with a woman twice my age! And where were you?

VI: I thought I was right *there*. *(Anger escalating)* What is it you girls want? You didn't get enough love? It wasn't the right kind? Wasn't unconditional? You weren't held enough, fed enough, disciplined enough, listened to enough, protected enough, liberated enough? Nothing was enough. Nothing is ever enough...never will be... *(Beat)* I guess we're just a massive disappointment to each other. *(Beat)* I can't protect you from bears in the night anymore.

JOANNA: She means big, black, beautiful bears that come in the night.

VI: That's the most racist thing I ever heard. You want me to give him up, Joanna? *Will that do it?* You want me to say I loved your father? *Will that do it?*

JOANNA: *(To VI)* Nothing will do it! *(Beat)* And F Y I, Cousin Eleanor is part Cuban. Aunt Ida did it with a guy from Cuba and never told Uncle Norman. That swarthy coloring, that gorgeous, dark hair and smooth as velvet thighs...

VI: *(Calling to BO)* Get me a glass of cognac.

(To JOANNA) You *are* involved with Cousin Eleanor.

JOANNA: I'm sorry, Ma. I am. After Phyllis, I decided Cousin Eleanor was a more grounded choice.

VI: You can't do that. First cousins are forbidden by law.

JOANNA: Only if you're heterosexual and having a baby together—which we may do. I'll carry the baby and Gary's offered his sperm. That would make Gary your double son-in-law.

VI: *(Turning C S)* With that, I saw my life unreeling in front of me like some old movie and the past was floating away like a scrap of paper.

JOANNA: We could do family counseling, Eleanor and I, you and Aunt Ida.

(BO *enters with cognac.*)

BO: Cognac anyone?

VI: Tell me something good. Anything

BO: Avery called before and he's coming over.

VI: Good. Tell me something else.

JOANNA: You're no longer responsible for us.

BO: Except for emergencies.

VI: How will I know what constitutes an emergency?

EMILY: We'll inform you.

VI: But what if you don't know you're in trouble, and *I* do? I just watch you go down the toilet?

BO: Maybe you watch, but don't flush... You aren't the one who's scared maybe there's no husband, nobody home, the summer looming ahead . Everything bad always happens in summer. School's out, Daddy left, camp stinks, and Eugene Larkin tried to sleep with me and I got scared and hid in the camp kitchen all night alone with a freezer full of ice cream. That's when the food thing really started. First it was the chocolate, then the coffee, then the rum raisin, then back to the chocolate, until it was morning and I was sick and went back to my bunk. *(Softly, almost a meltdown)* It's a true emergency. I swear.

VI: You'r2 wearing me down girls. *(Beat)* If you all could give me a small time out. I'm kind of beat...

EMILY: *(Entering)* Hey, guys! I almost forgot. The bagels! *(Opening her shopping bag, taking out bagels)* Anyone want a fresh bagel from Westchester?

VI: With a shmear.

BO: We're out of shmear. I finished it.

VI: Then what are you all waiting for? Go to the market and get some. What's a bagel without a shmear?

(The three girls exit as VI moves forward.)

VI: *(Out front)* I was on their side, only I was on my side too, and I couldn't figure out which side to stay on, so I had to keep jumping back and forth, which kept me on no side. I don't know what made me pick up that phone. You might say "choice". I would say it was my heart. I was about to give it all up. *(Then, picks up phone, punching in numbers)* This is Viola Davidson, and I know you'll understand, but a crisis has occurred, and the apartment won't be available after all. I'll return your deposit, with extra, and I apologize for this very unfortunate inconvenience. *(Hangs up, then goes over to computer, starts to type)* "My Dear Monsieur Orlion, It is with deep regret I must send you this letter and forfeit the opportunity to stay in your cottage, but I know you will understand that circumstances have changed for me this particular summer, beyond my control. Of course, I relinquish my deposit... *(Presses button on computer. Send. Out front)* ...Very late that same night...

(VI *then exits as* BO *enters in P Js , turns on light, sits on couch reading cookbook)*

(BO *is on the couch in her pajamas going through cookbooks.* GARY *enters in his bathrobe, holding a string of garlic in one hand and a pile of more cookbooks in the other.* GARY *puts the garlic up to* BO's *nose so she can smell it.)*

GARY: Fresh garlic is the ketchup of intellectuals.

(GARY *sits down beside her on the couch, not too far, almost touching. They through a stack of cookbooks.)*

BO: I say we start off with tatsoi and warm scallop salad with spicy pecan praline.

GARY: And I love the idea of the scallop salad because it uses avocado to balance the astringency of the greens.

BO: *And* the sharpness of the lemon.

(*Planning of the menu is like making love, each partner reaching a higher frenzy as they go on.)*

GARY: Served with a California Chardonnay.

BO: Say a Napa Valley Silver Label, delicate, but with a firm structure and a crispy but lush finish.

GARY: *Unless, unless* we do a warm salad of wood pigeon breasts with a gentle dusting of raspberry sauce.

BO: I don't know. People are squeamish about pigeon.

GARY: *Unless, unless,* we substitute mahi mahi , but then the dish loses it's integrity.

BO: Exactly. We'll stick with our tatsoi salad.

GARY: You know what would be dangerously provocative?

BO: Our lamb chop crepine with macerated apricots?

GARY: No, no! But you're getting hot!

BO: A whole roasted pig with individual pots of poupon mustard!

GARY: Hotter! Hotter! Give it to me, Baby! *(Beckoning to her and she comes closer)* Come on! Come on!

BO: *(Now, carried away by her excitement as the fever of joy rises, Bo ends up in* GARY's *lap)* Our pork tournadoes!

GARY: Over the moon! Now you're cooking, Momma!

(BO, *seeing where she's landed, removes herself from* GARY's *lap)*

GARY: But stuffed with...are you ready for this? Mango salsa!

BO: Be still my heart!

GARY: Wine with the second course?

BO: Hands down, a Reisling.

GARY: A '94 Nackenheimer Rothenberg.

BO: Adventuresome.

GARY: To die! The engaging fruit flavor and unexpected tittilation of power.

BO: YES! YES!

GARY: Oh oh.

BO: What?

GARY: Dessert. It has to be simple.

BO: Our broken glass cake.

GARY: But that's our private thing. And you can never count on it jelling. I think an uncomplicated creme brulee, flavored with cinnamon and served in a brown wicker basket with Medjool dates.

BO: Let's make the broken glass. It's risky, but I know I can do it. Oh Gary, I'm too excited to sleep. I feel like starting right now.

(Beat)

GARY: … You know, we *could* renew the lease and finish the book in Berkeley.

BO: Are you saying what I think you're saying?

GARY: I think that's what I'm saying.

BO: Then Muffy has to sleep in her perfectly good little dog bed. And no more food in the bedroom. And all the cookbooks off our night tables.

GARY: And no more T V. The only thing we watch anyway is the Food Channel.

BO: We could redo the bedroom, make it really romantic.

GARY: *(Beat)* I don't want to go up to bed without you.

BO: I know.

(GARY puts his arm around BO, they move towards the stairs)

GARY: I was thinking, if we finish the book by August...

(Sound of footsteps from upstairs)

GARY: Someone's up. Shh. They're in the bathroom.

(Beat, sound of toilet flushing)

GARY: Now they're flushing. *(Beat)* Now they're coming down the stairs.

(AVERY comes down stairs in pajamas and robe.)

GARY: Now they're here.

AVERY: I didn't think anyone was up.

BO: We couldn't sleep.

AVERY: Neither could I.

GARY: *(To AVERY)* Having an overnight I see. We were planning the birthday menu.

AVERY: I was going to make some warm milk.

ARNOLD: *(Entering, laden with packages)* I'd forgotten how enchanting malls are.

AVERY: The Sultan, I presume. *(Extending his hand)* I'm Avery.

GARY: If you'll excuse us, Sandman's calling.

BO: *(To* AVERY*)* Gary and I decided to go back to Berkeley. Mom will be thrilled. We'll announce it tomorrow night at her party.

GARY: *(As he exits upstairs)* I was thinking we could go to the Oxford Symposium on Food. This year's topic is "Endangered Foodstuffs and Disappearing Cuisines." The keynote address is by none other than Cherry Ripe, the Australian food critic.

ARNOLD: *(To* AVERY, *unpacking shopping bags)* It's epic. In one week I find out I'm going to be a father, reunite with my parents, and realize I love Emily more than the moon, and Emily and I are considering moving to Westchester with my parents. Vi will be so relieved. There's more room there. And we'd come down to the city all the time. *(Beat)* The truth is, we <u>are</u> moving. It will give us a real jump start, or as they say in Bali, *cepat jumlah.*

AVERY: *(To* ARNOLD*)* Good thing Vi didn't cancel her travel plans.

ARNOLD: Good thing.

*(*ARNOLD *exits up the stairs as* VI *passes him on the stairs, coming down in robe and slippers.)*

VI: I can't sleep.

AVERY: No one can sleep.

VI: I did it! I cancelled the house in Provence, and the rental. AND DON'T SAY A WORD! *(Beat)* I spoke with the Conductor and he called me something awful in Hungarian

AVERY: *(To* VI*)* But it must be what you want.

VI: It's not what I want.

AVERY: People around here are having a mighty hard time figuring out exactly what it is they *do* want...

VI: I just found my fingers typing, my hand on the phone, not a boundary in sight... *(Beat)* This has not been one of my more stellar days. I thought everything was going to turn out differently; —that my girls would be settled and normal, that no one I knew would go crazy and vote for movie stars for Governors. That I could put off turning sixty. *(Beat)* I did think that by now, someone would have carried me off to Paradise. Any volunteers?

(No volunteers as AVERY *leaves quietly and* VI *moves forward)*

VI: *(Out front)* The next morning I slept in, brought breakfast up to bed, then locked my door and played dead.

Then I took out all my old journals and read through my life trying to get a clue about how I got to this place... Then I set the table for dinner—the best china, crystal, the works.

*(*VI *moves to table, setting it for the birthday dinner the next night. Soon after,* AVERY *enters.)*

AVERY: Sorry. I thought I'd get away earlier.

VI: Why didn't you call?

AVERY: I don't own a cell phone.

VI: *Everyone* has a cell phone. They even have them in Outer Mongolia. Every sheepherder in Outer Mongolia has a cell phone and a Palm Pilot.

AVERY: Not me. I like pockets of unavailability.

VI: I'll try and remember that.

(AVERY *helps* VI *set the table. Everything* AVERY *puts down,* VI *picks up, changing it's position.*)

VI: Forks on the left.

AVERY: Good place for forks.

VI: You slipped out this morning before I got up.

AVERY: Early shoot…I have news.

VI: Good or bad?

AVERY: Good *and* bad. The big project I've been waiting on? It sailed in this afternoon. I'd all but kissed it goodbye. We *got* the *grant!* The one that's tied to the exhibit at the Met.

VI: Congratulations.

AVERY: Only glitch, we have to work nights when the museum's closed.

VI: Makes sense.

AVERY: Largest collection of Ming Dynasty pottery ever shown in America.

VI: So, this project at the Met, where you work at night…

AVERY: And prep during the day… *(Beat)* …You know, don't you.

VI: That even if I <u>was</u> going, you wouldn't be able to come now.

AVERY: You got it.

VI: So it's brilliant that I cancelled the plans! Because I always love New York in the summer, how the heat melts the sidewalks to butter, and the streets empty out, and you can get in almost anywhere, and the Yankees are always doing it....

(VI *turns on the C D player, starts to dance by herself. Intro, then Billie Holiday sings, mournful, sweet and slow*— What A Little Moonlight Can Do)

AVERY: Hold it, Vi!_Yes._ I'm in New York this summer, but once we dig into this, I might as well be in the Arctic.

(Now the lyrics begin...beat.

AVERY: It's Billie.

VI: An old recording.

AVERY: *(Joining* VI) Her at the Metropole—Roy Eldridge on trumpet, Coleman Hawkins on sax. *(Beat)* Look, they could just as well have called me in France and told me to fly to China.

VI: And the Norfolk Broads?

AVERY: On hold 'till fall. *(Beat)* But did the kids tell you?

VI: There's nothing much left they *could* tell me!

(VI *starts to sing along with the music, imitating Billie Holiday's sound and style ...)*

"Oh.....what a little moonlight can do ooh ooh, Oh what a little moonlight can be to you ..."

AVERY: Don't do that. *(Turns off C D)* Why don't you put on some Frank Sinatra.

VI: *(Turning on the C D again)* I don't like Sinatra.

AVERY: Please stay off my turf.

VI: I thought you'd like this.

AVERY: I do, but it's *my* music.

VI: You can't own music, and the reason I like Billie Holiday is she makes me feel good, because she makes me sad. *(She turns off C D)* It's the color thing, isn't it.

AVERY: What color thing?

VI: It is. You say it isn't, but it is.

AVERY: You're wrong. How do I say this? I like you, but The Met is big. You don't know when those assignments are going to come along. What I don't want is for someone to start counting on me.

VI: Which is what I wanted. I said I didn't, but I did.

AVERY: I try not to want. It gets me into trouble.

(At the same time, EMILY, ARNOLD, JOANNA *enter with great spirit, humming Mendelssohn's* Wedding March, *carrying a wrapped present.)*

JOANNA: So let the party begin!

EMILY: Bo and Gary have cooked up a storm. Used every pot in the house. Please be seated.

ARNOLD: *Wali songo.*

(All seat themselves, VI *at the head,* AVERY *next to her,* EMILY, ARNOLD, JOANNA.)

BO & GARY: *(From the other room)* Ready?

ALL: *(Seated at table)* Ready!

*(*BO *and* GARY *enter carrying a platter of scallops)*

GARY: Da da da da! *Le banquet commence.* Our tatsoi and warm scallop salad with spicy pecan praline sauce.

*(*GARY *holds the platter while* BO *serves each one.* VI *pours wine)*

EMILY: *(Holding up her wine glass)* To mother for her birthday. To her endless spirit of adventure.

(Each makes toast, holding glass up in turn.)

JOANNA: To the only original I know.

BO: Who taught her birds to always fly high.

AVERY: To Viola, who is bound by memory and freed by passion.

ARNOLD: Stunning.

GARY: *(Clears his throat, taps glass with knife)* Wait! We can't hold it in or we'll explode. You'll all be happy to know, *ta da*—Bo and I have decided to stay together.

BO: 'Till crumbs do us part.

GARY: We're going back to Berkeley to finish our book.

VI: You're not staying the summer?

BO: You know New York in the summer. It's deserted. Everyone's gone to the Hamptons or the Berkshires. There's no energy here in the summer.

EMILY: *(To* BO *and* GARY*)* Great news you two.

AVERY: *(Raising his glass)* And we lift our glasses to Viola, named for an instrument in the New York Philharmonic.

ARNOLD: Hear, hear! *(To* EMILY*)* Should we tell everyone *now*?

EMILY: We've decided to get married. An old-fashioned wedding. The whole thing. How does October sound? And don't kill us, Mom, but we're going to live with Titi's parents. There's really more room up there.
    They're swimming in room!

ARNOLD: Especially once the baby comes.

(Silence)

VI: Are you trying to tell me *no one needs to stay here this summer*?

EMILY: Really. It was ridiculous to expect you to give up everything just because we stamped our feet.

BO: *(To* VI *and* AVERY*)* Now you two can go to France like you planned.

VI: It turns out Avery has to stay in New York for the summer. And I cancelled the renter <u>and</u> the trip to Provence. *(Beat)* Well, you said you needed me.

EMILY: We say a lot of things.

BO: I feel awful. It's my fault.

GARY: It's probably mine.

AVERY: Could be mine.

ARNOLD: *Mea culpa.*

EMILY: Me too. *(To* JOANNA*)* That leaves you, Joanna.

JOANNA: I defer to Mother.

VI: *(Beat, looking to the right of her, then back)* I guess I
have no one left to defer to. *(Beat)* Can I tell you how
hard it is to cut the strings because then I fly solo?
(Beat) I'm calling France. Maybe the house is still
available. Or I'll rent another.

AVERY: You'll fall in love with France.

VI: I'd better fall in love with something.

GARY: What's burning?

BO: Oh no!

GARY: *(To* BO *as he runs into the kitchen)* The tournadoes!

*(*BO *follows* GARY *into kitchen.)*

(Smoke is bellowing out of the kitchen)

JOANNA: *(Following* GARY *into the kitchen)* Everyone
remain calm.

EMILY: *(To* ARNOLD*)* I feel nauseous.

(A nauseous EMILY *runs from the room,* ARNOLD *following
her)*

ARNOLD: *(As he exits)* It's the morning sickness. She
gets it at night.

JOANNA: *(Poking her head out of the kitchen)* Dinner will
be delayed while we scrape. *(Returns to kitchen)*

AVERY: You're a dangerous woman, Viola. You get people so distracted, the dinner burns. Your energy's seductive. You pull people in… You pull me in.

VI: But not far enough. *(Beat)* It's really ironic. New York.

AVERY: It is. But I think I have the perfect renter for you.

VI: I'm not calling back that abusive Hungarian.

AVERY: *I'll* rent it. I don't want to hike back to Queens every night. I get a good per diem. *(Beat)* And it's not the color thing.

VI: No. I don't think it is.

AVERY: It's my work.

VI: Of course. …Everyone seems to be getting out, mapping their own countries. Me? I'm not certain I even have a clear idea for my book.

AVERY: I don't think you're supposed to at the beginning.

VI: *(Her passion grows as she tells the story)* What I do have is notebooks. Thoughts. Kind of a first chapter. It's about this woman who moves to Ireland, and she's never really had a great love. Then she meets this man in Dublin. He breeds Irish setters...no, Russian wolfhounds. Russian wolfhounds are terribly complicated. They build a stone house by the sea. This all doesn't turn out well. I don't know why yet. *(Beat)* I'm calling that farmer in Provence, rapidment, to tell him I'm coming.

AVERY: The country code is thirty-three…And who knows? Maybe there's some research I'll have to do over there...and there I am.

VI: *(Her finger to her lips, "Shh")* Don't.

AVERY: Or I just come because I want to.

VI: Because I wow you.

AVERY: Because I want to be wowed.

VI: Careful. You're "wanting" something.... Did you know Russian wolfhounds, also known as borzois, were the favorites of Kings because of their aristocratic bearing. They hunt by sight, rather than smell.... My story will be about unexpected love, passion late in life, a gift of grace.

AVERY: And how will it turn out?

VI: That's a secret. I have my secrets, same as you.

(JOANNA *enters followed by* BO *and* GARY *carrying the burnt dinner with great aplomb.*)

JOANNA: Saved.

BO: Saved.

VI: Saved.

GARY: Bon appetite everyone.

VI: I have a call to make.

AVERY: Don't change your mind.

VI: *(Turning to exit)* Wild parasites couldn't keep me here... *(Then, out front)* So, by the end of that summer the girls had solved their problems, only to go on to new ones. I ended up renting to the Hungarian conductor and spent the summer in Provence writing my novel. Avery never did come, which was fine. The butcher in our little town was a genius at meat and rather cute.

And the story I wrote? It began like all beginnings... The world was all before them.

(Lights fade)

END OF PLAY

www.ingramcontent.com/pod-product-compliance
Lightning Source LLC
Chambersburg PA
CBHW070025110426
42741CB00034B/2603